May all your days
be filled with sunshine,
rainbows, & puppy kisses!

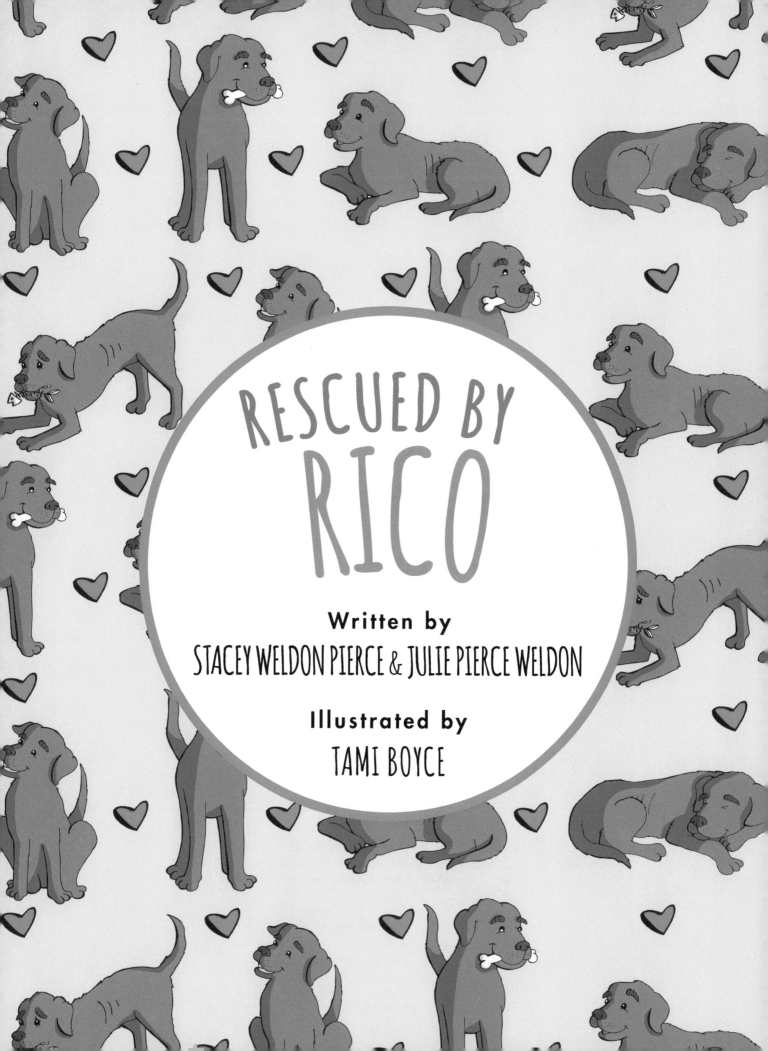

# RESCUED BY
# RICO

**Written by**

STACEY WELDON PIERCE & JULIE PIERCE WELDON

**Illustrated by**

TAMI BOYCE

*A portion of the proceeds from the sale of this book will go to support dog rescue missions that are doing great work.*

ISBN-13: 978-1-7352763-0-4

A Salty Rim Publishing
Charleston, SC

Edited by Susan Burlingame

*"**Rescued By Rico**" is dedicated to all those heroes who rescue fur babies. It is also dedicated with love to all of us who have had to watch our precious pets cross over the Rainbow Bridge.*

"SAVING ONE DOG WILL NOT CHANGE THE WORLD,
BUT SURELY FOR THAT ONE DOG,
THE WORLD WILL CHANGE FOREVER."
—KAREN DAVISON

Not very long ago, there was a very, very big storm in Puerto Rico. The wind howled. The rain poured out of the sky in buckets. Lightning flashed over and over and over. Thunder boomed. The storm was so bad and so dangerous that people had to leave their homes to seek shelter.

And that's how Rico, a very nice brown dog, found himself all alone.

"I guess my family left me to protect the house," Rico thought to himself.

But days, weeks, and even months passed. More storms came and went. Rico searched and searched for his family, but he soon realized they were not coming back.

"I'm so hungry!" Rico cried. "What am I going to do?"

Luckily, Rico was a very smart pup, so he found ways to survive. He would eat scraps out of trash cans or find bits of food in other abandoned houses. It wasn't easy living on the streets for poor Rico.

And he wasn't alone. There were lots of pups just like him. Hungry and sad and tired. Scrounging for food.

One day, when Rico was extra sad and hungry, he decided to take a nap to forget his troubles. After a while, he heard a soft voice and awoke to the sight of a blonde-haired girl. She was smiling and holding out her hand. To Rico, she looked like an angel.

"Hi, little fella," said the girl. "I'm Shanna. Would you like something to eat?"

Shanna had a giant heart, and she loved helping lost and hungry dogs, so she put some food on the floor where Rico lay.

"I must be dreaming," thought Rico. But he wasn't dreaming! Shanna had brought him real food! Rico was almost too weak to lift his head to eat, but somehow he managed to gobble up the delicious snack—his first real meal in so, so long.

While Rico ate his food, Shanna stroked his matted fur. She could tell he hadn't been brushed or loved for a very long time.

"Poor little fella," said Shanna. Rico closed his eyes and remembered the family he used to have.

"Maybe Shanna will be my new person,"
Rico hoped. But it wasn't to be. Shanna petted Rico and stood up.
"Oh, please don't go!" Rico cried. But of course, Shanna didn't
understand because she didn't speak dog language. She smiled and
turned to walk away.
"Don't worry, little fella," said Shanna. "I'll be back tomorrow."
But of course, Rico didn't understand either.
Though he was very sad, Rico had a full belly for the first time in
many months. He slept peacefully and dreamed of Shanna... and food.

The next morning, Rico opened his sleepy eyes. He blinked. Then he blinked again. Was he still dreaming?? No, it wasn't a dream. Shanna was back!!

"Hello again, little fella!" said Shanna. "Will you come along with me? I'm going to find you a new home and family."

What Rico didn't know was that he had completely captured Shanna's heart. She was a dog rescuer who helped lost pups in Puerto Rico find new homes, so she posted a picture of Rico on the internet, and a very special couple in Charleston, South Carolina wanted to adopt him. She also contacted a friend, a dog rescuer who was the assistant to a famous country star. Shanna's friend said that help was on its way.

Shanna gently lifted Rico into her arms. A new life for Rico was about to begin.

In the meantime, Shanna gave Rico plenty of food and water. She took him to the beach to play and gave him a plush bed to sleep on when he got tired. She took him to the animal doctor, who said that though Rico was old and sick and skinny, he deserved to have a good life.

"I am so happy," thought Rico. "I was all alone, and I was so hungry and tired, but now someone loves me again."

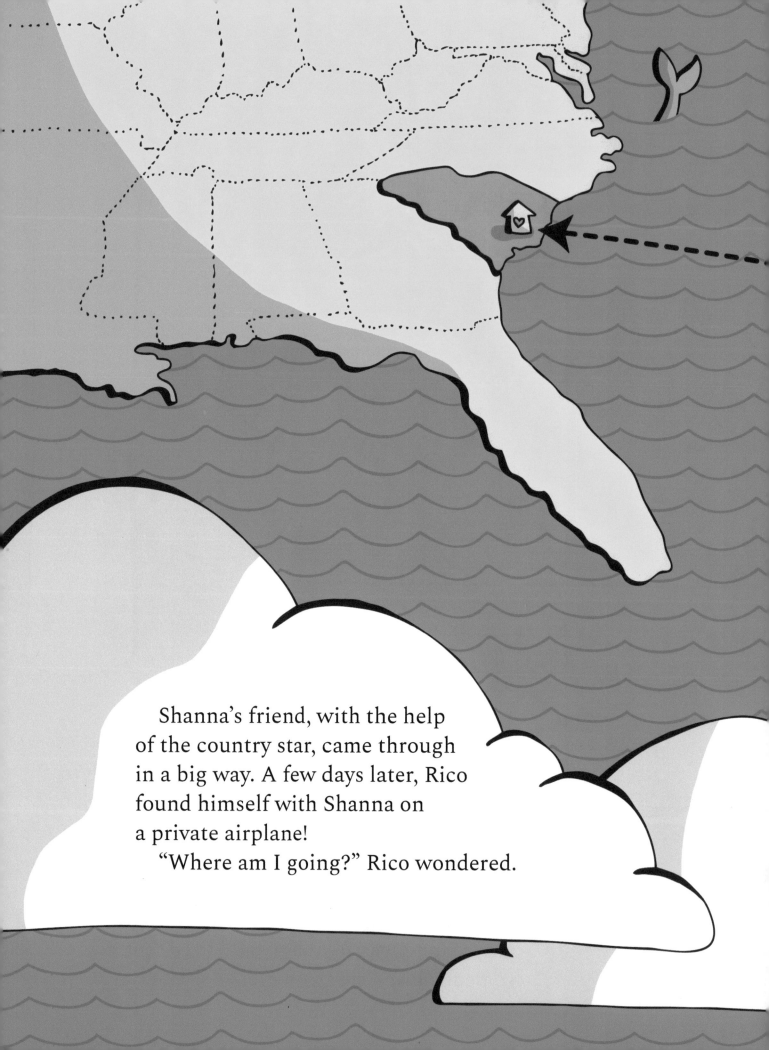

Shanna's friend, with the help of the country star, came through in a big way. A few days later, Rico found himself with Shanna on a private airplane!

"Where am I going?" Rico wondered.

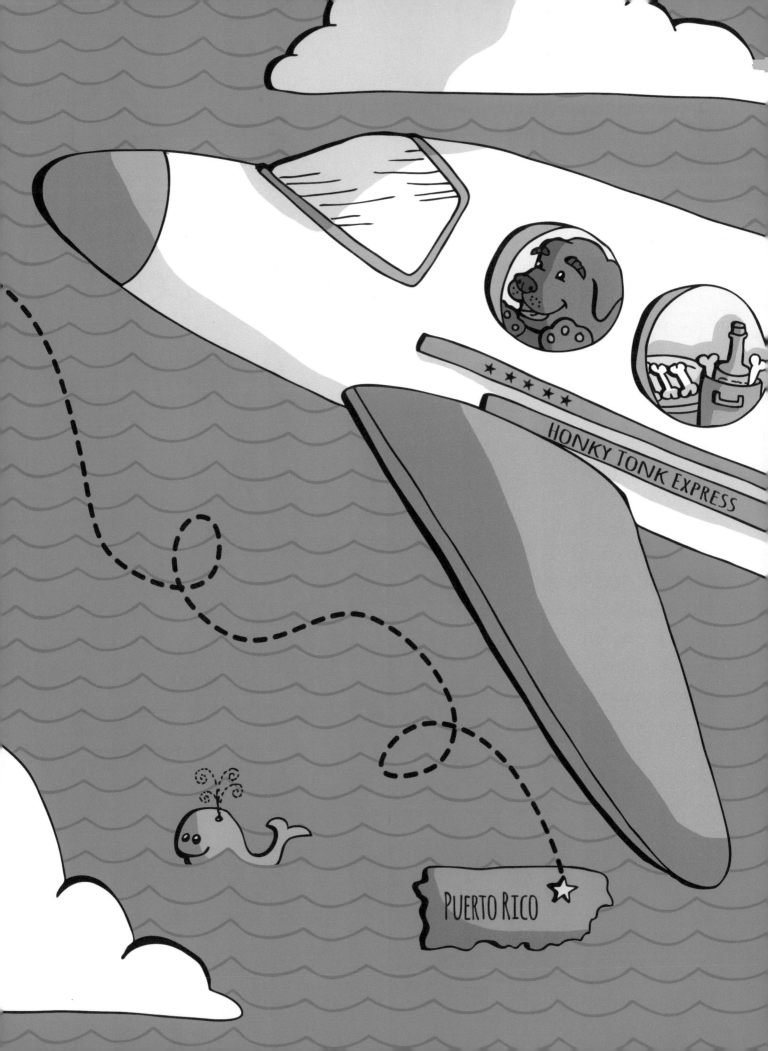

Shanna and Rico landed in Charleston, where Rico's new people were waiting to greet him.

"Meet your new moms—Jules and Stace," Shanna said.

Two smiling women hugged and petted Rico. "Welcome to your new home!" said Stace.

"Let's call him 'Rico!'" said Jules. After all, Rico had come all the way from Puerto Rico to live with them. It didn't matter that he was old and sick and skinny. It didn't matter that they already had another dog. Rico had captured their hearts, and Jules and Stace were determined to give him a wonderful life for as long as they could.

PUPPY YUMMERS

PUPPY YUMMERS

Rico was stunned and happy, but there was another surprise in store for him. The prettiest pup Rico had ever seen – another dog rescued by Jules and Stace – greeted him with a wagging tail and a doggy kiss right on the nose!

"Meet Lucy! Your new friend!" said Shanna.

And then it was time for Shanna to go. "Goodbye, little fella," she said, as she gave Rico one more hug. "I'm so glad we found you a new home and a new family."

Shanna turned to go, promising she would visit often.

Rico was sad to see Shanna leave, but he knew he would be ok. He was scared and nervous a lot, especially at night, but he soon learned to love his new family, especially Lucy. The two dogs talked to each other in dog language about the old sad days and how they were both so happy now. They became inseparable, playing together...

Napping together...

Eating together...

And even sharing a water bowl
every morning, where they
would greet each other
with a kiss.

"We are so lucky," said Stace to Jules one morning. "Rico is such a sweet boy. I bet he was loved very much by his first family. To think we didn't want a second dog!"

"I know!" answered Jules. "Rico has made our family even more complete. I think he's the one who rescued US — not the other way around!"

Jules and Stace both knew that Rico was very old and might not have a long life, but they made sure it was a happy one. One day, they decided they should tell Rico about the Rainbow Bridge.

"One day you will be so tired that you will decide to sleep forever," they told him. "On that day, you will see a beautiful bridge that looks just like a rainbow. When you cross that bridge, you will see all your old friends. You will feel young and healthy, and you will have all the treats and toys you could ever want."

Rico seemed to understand.

One day, about five months after Rico came to live with Jules and Stace and Lucy, he felt very, very sleepy and weak. "I think I'm ready to cross the Rainbow Bridge," Rico said to himself. He kissed Lucy goodbye, enjoyed one more loving hug from Jules and Stace, and closed his eyes.

And there it was! The Rainbow Bridge. Bright and shiny and beautiful...and full of dogs and cats and bunnies! Some of them were holding signs that said "Welcome home, Rico!"

Rico wagged his tail and ran toward his friends, content that he had a wonderful life and was about to begin a new one.

THE END

# THE TRUE STORY OF RICO

*We were honored to be Rico's parents for the few short months he lived after joining our little family. In our minds, we believe he gave us much more than we gave him. Here is how it happened that a sweet, abandoned pup from Puerto Rico came to live with us.*

## —Jules and Stace

While visiting Puerto Rico after Hurricane Maria had devastated the island in 2017, our friend, Shanna, a dog lover and dog rescuer, spotted a chocolate Labrador retriever lying on the floor of a restaurant. He looked very skinny and sick, so Shanna ordered him chicken and gave him her lunch while shedding tears. After the dog ate, he laid down at Shanna's feet, instantly winning over Shanna's heart. Shanna vowed to do something to help. With permission from the restaurant owner, Shanna took the poor dog and set out to find him a home.

Shanna took the dog to a veterinarian in San Juan and found out he was between 12-14 years old. He was 20 pounds underweight and had a litany of health issues. The vet said Rico didn't have much time to live but hoped he would be loved and cared for in the meantime. Shanna vowed to make sure of it.

Shanna posted about Rico on her Facebook page, and we fell in love with him the moment we saw his sweet face. We knew he belonged with us and our other rescue dog, Lucy. Shanna contacted her friends, Jessica and Jill, who helped make it possible to fly Rico on two private planes (he was too sick to fly commercial) to Charleston, South Carolina, where we live. After the plane rides, Shanna drove Rico nine hours to meet us. We named him "Rico" to honor where he had come from and what he had been through.

There were some very difficult moments as Rico learned to trust that we weren't going to abandon him. But Rico was meant for us, and we were meant for Rico. We named our book "Rescued by Rico" because he made such an impact on our lives. He fit in like he had been ours all along, and our Lucy absolutely adored him. Rico was a gentle soul, and we were only too happy to give him a loving home for the five short months he had left in his life. Rico crossed the Rainbow Bridge on the morning of August 6, 2018, knowing he was loved.

*Sadly, it is estimated that over one million dogs are homeless in Puerto Rico as a result of the hurricane. Helping even one makes a tremendous difference—both for the dogs and for the families who adopt them. We received an amazing gift that lasted five wonderful months, and we have Shanna's big heart to thank for our time with Rico. For more information about saving abandoned dogs in Puerto Rico, visit El Faro de los Animales online at elfaropr.org, Big Dog Ranch Rescue at bdrr.org, or the Animal Care Center of St. John at stjohnanimalcarecenter.com. Our sincerest gratitude to Shanna Dickerson, Jill Trunnell, and Jessica Nicodemo, who came together to find help and a home for Rico.*

# MEET THE AUTHORS, ILLUSTRATOR, & COPY EDITOR

**JULES AND STACE** live in Charleston, South Carolina. They love life and are always in pursuit of fun and memorable experiences. As such, they are business coaches/ consultants with their company, A Salty Rim. They host two podcasts — GSD Entrepreneur and Do It In Nature, and they have an outdoor gear company called OME Gear. You can often find them enjoying the beach or hiking in the mountains. They love rescue pups and fell in love with Rico the moment they first saw him. They immediately knew he belonged with them and their other rescue pup, Lucy, who ended up being the love of Rico's life.

**TAMI BOYCE**, an illustrator and graphic designer with a fun and whimsical style, is based in Charleston, South Carolina.

"Holding a pencil in my hand has been my passion for as long as I can remember. I count myself as an extremely lucky individual because I have been able to make a career out of it. We all live in a very serious world, and I like to use my quirky style to remind us of the love, joy, and humor that is often overlooked around us."

To see more of Tami's work, visit tamiboyce.com.

**SUSAN BURLINGAME** is a freelance writer and editor for children's books and a variety of other publications. She has always loved words and delights in helping storytellers bring their stories to life. Based in central Pennsylvania, Susan also is a full-time writer for a local university and a singer and guitarist for several local bands. To contact Susan, send an email to sjbwords@gmail.com.

CPSIA information can be obtained
at www.ICGtesting.com
Printed in the USA
LVHW071950170920
666399LV00001B/1